OUR AMAZING CONTINENTS

Continents are the largest pieces of land
on Earth. There are seven continents.
The largest is Asia. The other continents,
from largest to smallest, are Africa,
North America, South America, Antarctica,
Europe, and Australia. Each continent's
landscape has shaped the lives of its
animals, plants, and people.

Library of Congress Cataloging-in-Publication Data

Sayre, April Pulley.
G'day, Australia! / April Pulley Sayre.
      p. cm. — (Our amazing continents)
Summary: Introduces the continent of Australia, looking at its
geography, plant and animal life, weather, and settlement by humans.
   ISBN 0-7613-2122-5 (lib. bdg.)   ISBN 0-7613-1987-5 (pbk.)
   1. Australia—Juvenile literature. [1. Australia.] I. Title.
DU96 .S28 2003
994—dc21
2002015676

Front cover photograph courtesy of Animals Animals (© Gerard Lacz);
back cover courtesy of Bruce Coleman, Inc. (© Daniel Zupanc/ZUPAN)

Photographs courtesy of Photo Researchers, Inc.: pp. 1 (© PLI/SPL), 3 (© Bill Bachman), 16
(© Tom McHugh), 18-19, 20 (© Wayne Lawler); Bruce Coleman, Inc.: pp. 4 (© Erwin &
Peggy Bauer), 5 (top © John Giustina; bottom © Mark Newman), 8 (© Daniel Zupanc-
Austria), 11 (© Erwin & Peggy Bauer), 12 (bottom © John Shaw), 28 (top © Andria Apse;
bottom © C.B & B.W. Frith), 30-31 (© M.P. Fogden); Photri, Inc.: p. 6; Corbis: pp. 9 (© Paul
A. Souders), 15 (© Stephanie Colasanti), 21 (© Clive Druette/Papilio), 22 (© Paul A.
Souders), 29 (© Penny Tweedie); Peter Arnold, Inc.: pp. 10-11 (© Auscape); Visuals
Unlimited, Inc.: pp. 12 (top © Joe McDonald), 24 (top © Robert E. Barber), 24-25 (©
Neville Coleman); Animals Animals: pp. 13 (© Fritz Prenzel), 23 (top: © Klaus Uhlenhut;
bottom: © Hans & Judy Beste), 24 (bottom © Gowlett-Holmes, OSF), 31 (© Hans & Judy
Beste); Australian Tourist Commission: p. 26. Map on p. 32 by Joe LeMonnier.

Published by The Millbrook Press, Inc.
2 Old New Milford Road
Brookfield, Connecticut 06804

Western Australia: Pilbara Region

G'DAY,
AUSTRALIA!

APRIL PULLEY SAYRE

THE MILLBROOK PRESS BROOKFIELD, CONNECTICUT

Kangaroo with joey in pouch

Where do kangaroos hop?

Where do wombats dig?

Where do dingoes run and play?

Wombat

In Australia—

where you can find some of the world's most unusual animals.

Dingoes

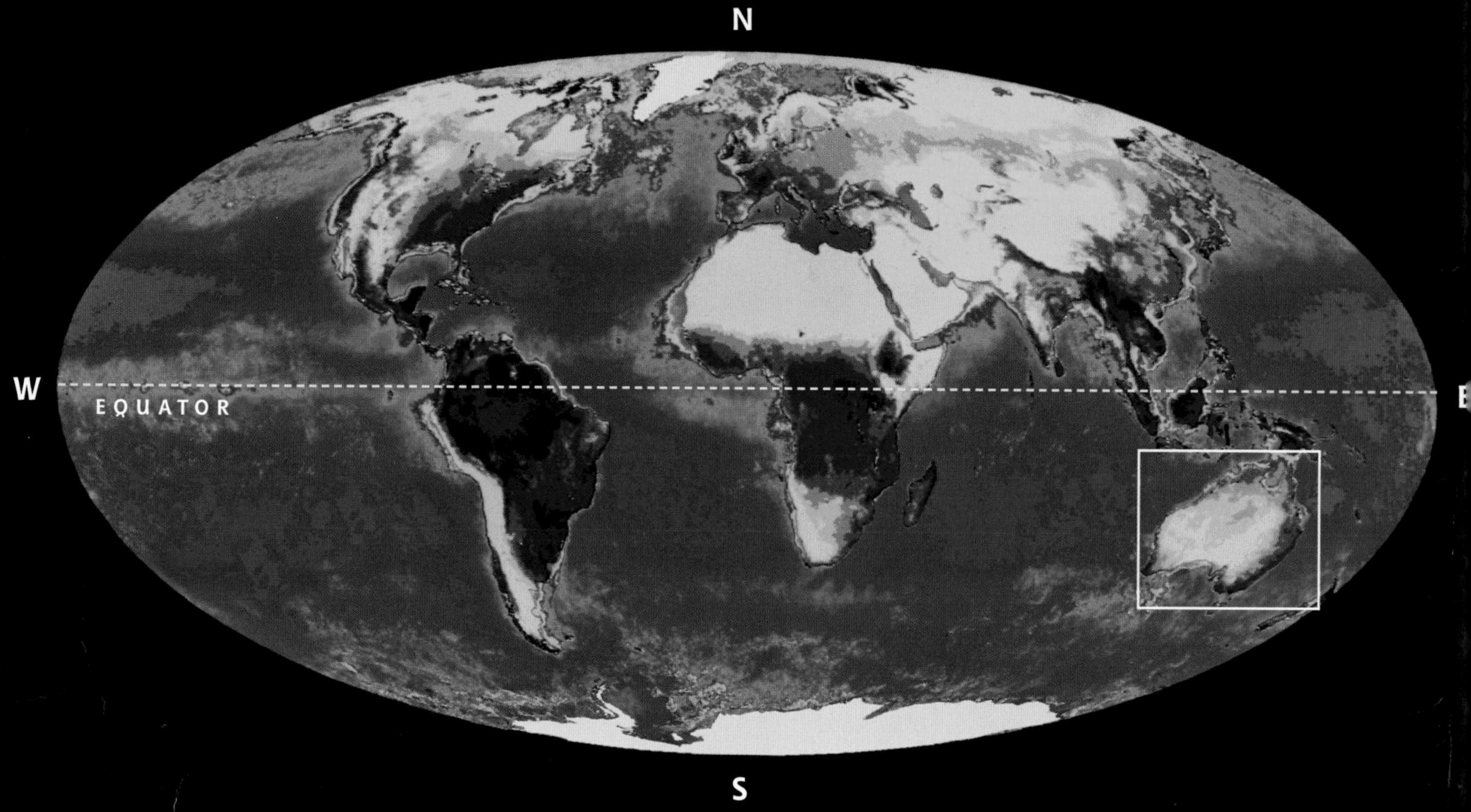
N
W
EQUATOR
E
S

Australia is the smallest continent.

Some people call it "the Land Down Under" because it is in the Southern Hemisphere. The Southern Hemisphere is south of the equator, an imaginary line around Earth's middle.

Australia lies between the Indian Ocean and the Pacific Ocean.

Elabana Falls, Queensland.

Recess at a school outside Canberra

Australia is also the name of a country.

Most continents are divided into many countries. Australia is not. The country Australia covers the entire Australian continent.

Australia has six states and two territories. The states are: Queensland, South Australia, Western Australia, New South Wales, Tasmania, and Victoria. The territories are the Northern Territory and the Australian Capital Territory, where the capital city, Canberra, is located.

Lake Hanson, a glacial lake

The state of Tasmania is an island.

Tasmania is located off the southeast coast of Australia. The country of New Zealand is also an island near Australia. But New Zealand is not part of the Australian continent.

Tasmania has beautiful lakes, rivers, mountains, and rain forests. Tasmania is home to the Tasmanian devil, an animal about the size of a small dog. This animal is a marsupial, a mammal with a pouch to carry its young.

Tasmanian Devil

Rock Wallabies

Koala in a eucalyptus tree

Australia is famous for its unique animals.

Many of Australia's animals do not live anywhere else in the world. Most of the world's marsupials live in Australia. Kangaroos, wombats, wallabies, and koalas are marsupials. The koala is Australia's national symbol.

Platypus

Another odd Australian animal is the platypus.

Platypuses have webbed feet and a bill like a duck. Their bodies are covered with fur. Platypuses are monotremes. Monotremes are mammals that lay eggs. Another Australian animal, the echidna, is a monotreme, too.

Australia is flat.

Australia is the flattest continent. It has very few mountains. The mountains it does have are not very high. Australia's one major mountain range is called the Great Dividing Range. It goes from north to south along the eastern edge of the continent.

A valley between the mountains of the Great Dividing Range.

Australia is the second-driest continent.

Dingoes cool off in the water of a billabong.

Only Antarctica is drier than Australia.

Much of Australia is desert and semi-desert, where little or no rain falls. Australians call these areas "the outback." Australia has very few lakes and rivers and many of these are dry part of each year. When the rivers begin to dry up, they leave behind pools of water called billabongs. Billabongs are important drinking holes for wildlife.

Bondi beach in the city of Sydney

Australia has modern cities, crowded with people.

But every other continent, except Antarctica, has more people than Australia. There are more sheep in Australia than there are people. Cattle and sheep ranches in the outback are so big that some ranchers use planes and helicopters to keep track of their animals. In the outback you can travel for days without seeing another person. Children who live there have school at home, and contact their teacher by two-way radio, computer, telephone, and fax machine.

Australia has many savannas.

Savannas are grasslands with widely spaced trees. Australians call savannas and brushy areas "the bush." Many kinds of trees and bushes in the eucalypt family grow in Australia. Some smell like eucalyptus cough drops.

Laughing kookaburras, a kind of kingfisher, often perch in eucalypt trees.

A kookaburra

These birds are named for their call, which sounds like human laughter. Kangaroos in herds, called mobs, graze on the savannas. Dingoes, Australia's wild dogs, travel in groups, called packs. They hunt sheep, kangaroos, and rabbits.

Sydney Harbor

Australia also has cooler, wetter areas near the coasts.

Most Australians live in the coastal areas. Australia's large cities, such as Sydney and Melbourne, are on its southern and eastern coasts.

Rain forest

Ringtail possum

Australia has some even wetter places: rain forests. These rain forests are up in its mountains. Frogs, bowerbirds, parrots, and possums live in the rain forests. Male bowerbirds make a special stage, called a bower. They decorate it with feathers, flowers, and other colorful and shiny objects. This helps attract females.

Sea snake

Along one coast is the Great Barrier Reef.

The Great Barrier Reef is Earth's largest coral reef. It is made of many smaller reefs. A coral reef is an underwater ridge. It is made of the skeletons of tiny sea animals. Colorful fish, sea stars, octopuses, sea snakes, sharks, and other creatures live in a reef.

Biscuit Sea stars

Christmas at the beach

Australia's location affects its seasons.

Because Australia is in the Southern Hemisphere, its seasons are the opposite of those in the Northern Hemisphere. In Australia, summer starts in December. At Christmastime, the weather is so hot many Australians go the the beach! Schools close for the month of January for summer vacation. Winter begins in June.

Aborigines in the Northern Territory

The people who first lived in Australia were Aborigines.

They have lived in Australia for 40,000 years. Their descendants live in Australia today. Aborigines have a rich culture and traditions. Their songs, stories, and religion are deeply connected to the Australian land.

Playing a didgeridoo

An Aborigine musical instrument is called a didgeridoo.

The best ones are made from eucalypt tree trunks hollowed by termites.

Uluru

Australia contains some of the oldest rocks on Earth.

Those rocks are three billion years old. Some of the most famous rock forms are Uluru, the Twelve Apostles, and the Bungle Bungles.

Uluru is in the middle of the continent. It is huge — almost 2 miles (3.2 kilometers) long. Many tourists like to climb to the top of this beautiful rock. Uluru shines reddish and pinkish in the sunlight. Uluru is a sacred place to the Australian Aborigines. Australia is an ancient and wondrous continent.

Twelve Apostles

How do you get to know the face of a continent?

AUSTRALIA

ASIA

TIMOR SEA

Bungle Bungles

Northern Territory

North Queens-land

Great Barrier Reef

CORAL SEA

Pilbara Region

Uluru

GREAT DIVIDING RANGE

Tropic of Capricorn

PACIFIC OCEAN

Elabana Falls

● Sydney
● Canberra

Twelve Apostles

INDIAN OCEAN

Lake Hanson

Tasmania

New Zealand

0   400 miles

0   600 kilometers

KEY
Outback
Rain Forest
Humid
Savanna

Books are one way. This book is about the natural features of a continent. Maps are another way. You can discover the heights of mountains and the depths of valleys by looking at a topographical map. A political map will show you the outlines of countries and locations of cities and towns.

Globes are a third way to learn about the land you live on. Because globes are Earth-shaped, they show more accurately how big the continents are, and where they are. Maps show an Earth that is squashed flat, so the positions and sizes of continents are slightly distorted. A globe can help you imagine what an astronaut sees when looking at our planet from space. Perhaps one day you'll fly into space and see it for yourself! Then you can gaze down at the brown faces of continents, and the blue of the oceans, and the white clouds floating around Earth.